Selected Poems

Anna Akhmatova

Selected Poems

Translated with an Introduction by
Richard McKane

and an essay by
Andrei Sinyavsky

London
Oxford University Press
New York Toronto
1969

Oxford University Press, Ely House, London W.1
Glasgow New York Toronto Melbourne
Wellington Cape Town Salisbury Ibadan Nairobi
Lusaka Addis Ababa Bombay Calcutta Madras
Karachi Lahore Dacca Kuala Lumpur Singapore
Hong Kong Tokyo

891.7
A

First published by Oxford University Press, 1969
Simultaneously published in paperback by
Penguin Books Ltd., 1969

Printed in Great Britain

Contents

Acknowledgement

The poems in this book are translated from
original versions given in *Anna Akhmatova,
Works*, Vol. 1, Inter-Language Literary
Associates, 1967.

Introduction

Anna Andreevna Gorenko was born in June 1889 at Bolshoi Fontan, a suburb of Odessa on the Black Sea. Her father was a retired naval engineer. She took her *nom de plume* 'Akhmatova' from her grandmother. Most of her early life was spent in the St Petersburg area, first in Pavlovsk, then in Tsarskoe Selo (see notes p. 15), but she used to return to the Black Sea for her summer holidays. In 1907 she finished her secondary education in Kiev and started a course in law at the Kiev College for Women. But she lost interest in academic work and returned to St Petersburg, where she was to live most of her life. In 1910 she married the poet Nikolai Gumilyov. In 1918, shortly after Gumilyov's return from France where he had been serving with the Russian expeditionary force, they were divorced. Akhmatova subsequently remarried twice. In 1921 Gumilyov was shot for alleged conspiracy in an anti-Bolshevik plot in Petrograd. His name appeared in a list of sixty-one names including a handful of intellectuals, some officers and sailors, peasants and workers. They were all executed on or around 24 August 1921.

Akhmatova stayed in Leningrad until 1941, and was evacuated from the city with a few other writers only when it was already blockaded by the Germans. She lived in Tashkent for three years and returned to Leningrad in June 1944. She had visited Paris in 1910 and 1911, where she was drawn by Modigliani. In 1912 she went to Italy and over fifty years later she returned to receive the Etna-Taormina poetry prize. The following year she went to Oxford to receive an honorary doctorate. She died in March 1966.

Akhmatova's first collection of poems, *Evening*, was published in 1912 in an edition of 300 copies. In 1914 *Rosary*, her second collection, established her position and popularity. *White Flock* followed in 1917, then a small collection, *Plantain*, in 1921. This last collection was included in *Anno Domini*, published in full in 1923. She published no poetry between 1925 and 1940 but we can ascribe to this period a fragment of a long poem, some thirty lyrics and the early poems which belong to the 'Requiem' cycle. At this time Akhmatova studied Pushkin and the architecture of old St Petersburg. In 1940 an edition of her earlier work was published; although this omitted a number of earlier poems, particularly those with religious symbols and images, it did include another book, *Willow* (see p. 71; this title was later changed to *Reed*).

In 1912 Akhmatova and her first husband, Nikolai Gumilyov, became founder members of the Acmeist movement and, with Osip Mandelshtam, were its leading figures. Gumilyov was the leader of the Poets' Guild, as the Acmeist movement was also called. By 1910 Symbolism was no longer a coherent force in Russian poetry; a conflict had developed inside the movement between Bryusov and his followers and Bely, Blok and Vyacheslav Ivanov, who considered that Symbolism was almost a mystical religion.

Acmeism placed a greater importance on sense than

on sounds and insisted on clarity rather than the vague images to which the Symbolists had been prone. The poetry of Mandelshtam is especially rich in classical themes, from the Homeric to the Roman. In Gumilyov and Akhmatova we also see this (pp. 83–4) but to a much smaller extent. At the same time as Akhmatova, Gumilyov and Mandelshtam were testing the possibilities of Acmeism, the Futurist movement was developing in a separate way. Vladimir Mayakovsky, the greatest Futurist poet, needed new words, new rhythms, new heights of exaggeration to convey the oversize world he saw. But Akhmatova looked back to a traditional lyric vocabulary and traditional themes which had been cultivated by the poets Pushkin (1799–1837) and Tyutchev (1803–73).

It was Osip Mandelshtam who pointed to Akhmatova's 'genesis in Russian prose': 'Akhmatova brought to the Russian lyric the wealth of the Russian novel of the nineteenth century.' He mentions especially her debt to Dostoyevsky. In Akhmatova's 'Prehistory' (which is connected with the Northern Elegies, pp. 86–9) the poet compares her Leningrad with the old St Petersburg, which played such an important part in the works of Pushkin, Gogol, Dostoyevsky and Goncharov:

> But the city has changed little.
> Not I alone, but others also
> have noticed that it can sometimes
> resemble an old lithograph
> of – it seems – the seventies.
>
> *Dostoyevsky's Russia*

The strength of Akhmatova's love poems lies in the tension between the underlying emotion and the

9

descriptive setting: the clarity and sharpness of definition of objects, the freezing of time, which heighten or create the emotion of a particular situation between the poet and her lover. The theme which Akhmatova treats with most originality is that of parting, an experience she had tested to the full in her private life. In 1934 her son, Lev Gumilyov, was arrested on a charge which has never been fully revealed. He was soon released but in 1937 was arrested again, and only released during the war to fight in the army. He returned home in 1945. In the autumn of 1949 he was rearrested and finally released in May 1956. Most of this time he spent in concentration camps. 'Requiem' is a cycle of poems written as a memorial to the poet's own personal suffering and to the suffering of millions of others. It is her most powerful and logical development of the themes of love, parting and suffering. It triumphantly vindicates the prophetic judgement of the critic, Kornei Chukovsky, who wrote in 1921, in an essay in *Dom Iskusstv*: 'From her first book it was obvious that she was the poet of the orphans, the widows; that her poetry was nourished on the feeling of lack of possession, parting and loss.'

During the war Akhmatova continued to write poems while evacuated to Central Asia. The war had given artists more freedom of expression, but in 1946 the situation changed. There had been murmurings against the satirist Zoshchenko in earlier years but on 14 August he and Akhmatova were singled out for attack. In a decree in *Pravda* the Central Committee ordered the magazine *Leningrad* to cease publication, severely reprimanded *Zvezda*, and ordered that they should have nothing to do with Akhmatova and

Zoshchenko. The attack on Akhmatova was reinforced by the personal intervention of Zhdanov, who was tipped as the possible successor to Stalin. Akhmatova's themes of love and religion and her highly personal poetry were peculiarly vulnerable to attack from Zhdanov, who demanded that literature serve the state. He claimed that 'mists of loneliness and hopelessness alien to Soviet literature run through the whole history of Akhmatova's "creative" work.' Zhdanov used Akhmatova and Zoshchenko as scapegoats and his treatment of them was calculated to stamp out any opposition among the intelligentsia. The effect of Zhdanov's attack was to stop Akhmatova's literary output dead until 1950, and effectively to silence the literary world. In September 1946 both Akhmatova and Zoshchenko were expelled from the Writers' Union.

During this period Akhmatova turned to translation, which was less likely to arouse controversy, and she translated mainly from the Serbian and the Korean. In 1950 her poems began again to appear in periodicals. But 'Requiem' was first published outside the U.S.S.R., in Munich in 1963, 'without the knowledge and consent of the author'. The final text of 'Poem Without a Hero' was published in London in July 1967 in the *Slavonic and East European Review*, although earlier incomplete versions had appeared in the U.S.S.R. and the U.S.A. Akhmatova worked on 'Poem Without a Hero' on and off from 1940 to 1962. It is her longest and most difficult poem. Its complexity and allusions demand a detailed knowledge of the way of life of the poet and her friends which put it beyond the scope of this selection. From the early 1950s, and especially after the 20th Party Congress of 1956, when Khrushchev denounced Stalin, Akhmatova was allowed to publish poetry and she gradually became reaccepted on the literary scene. Finally, in 1964, she became President of the Union of Writers.

The Etna-Taormina poetry prize and the Oxford honorary doctorate helped make her name better known in the West. They also confirmed the world's belief that Anna Akhmatova was the greatest living Russian poet.

Oxford, 1968   RICHARD MCKANE

The Unshackled Voice

For years Akhmatova's poetry appeared locked, frozen within the limits set by her early books – *Evening, Rosary, White Flock*. Living in the past, in her private world and in her own poetic tradition, she seemed the prisoner of her own familiar themes, chosen intonations, long-discovered images from which she would never break away. That Akhmatova was 'destined to repeat herself' was said by critics as early as the 1920s, and unfortunately this old impression still survives in the mind of the public.

Yet, if we turn to the Akhmatova of today and re-read what she has written in the past three decades, we are struck by many new, decisive notes, unexpected, bold developments, quite out of keeping with our long-established view of her character as a poet.

> The harsh epoch
> turned me back like a river.
> My life has been secretly changed,
> and flows
> along another course,
> past other landmarks,
> and I do not know my banks.

While remaining true to herself, this new Akhmatova forces us to discard the established image of her as merely a pre-revolutionary poet, narrow in scope and

set in her ways. To begin with, this is glaringly dis-
proved by the poems, full of tragic power and courage,
written in the 1930s and in wartime. Akhmatova argues
with those who would like to see her as an uncommitted
person, estranged from the life of her own country and
uninterested in the fate of the people. It is enough to take
these lines about the years of the Yezhovshchina, years
of personal tragedy for Akhmatova herself.*

> No – not under the vault of another sky,
> not under the shelter of other wings.
> I was with my people then,
> there where my people were doomed to be.

Her wartime poetry, where artist and citizen are so
clearly at one, rings with high courage and compassion:

> We know what now lies on the scales
> and what is happening now.
> The hour of courage has struck for us
> and courage will not desert us.
> We have no fear in facing the bullets,
> no bitterness in being left without homes,
> and we will treasure you our Russian speech,
> the great Russian word.
> Pure and free we will uphold you
> and give you to our descendants,
> and save you from bondage forever.

Akhmatova's poetry has changed in its very structure,
its very sound. We thought of it as muted, delicate,
feminine and fragile, we followed the play of half-tones,
of 'motes', of barely audible, barely perceptible modu-

*The worst years of the purges in the 1930s, when Yezhov was
head of the NKVD, and when Akhmatova's husband was shot
and her son imprisoned. Also see note to p. 90.

14

lations. But who would have believed that this Royal Village Muse* could talk so loud, so big, in the language of the street and of the market place – and in speaking of the Royal Village itself, thrice sung and for so long the very symbol of the refined poetic language of the past?

> There the soldiers' jokes flow
> with undiminished venom.
> A striped sentry box,
> and a stream of tobacco smoke.
> They bawled out songs
> and swore at the priest's wife,
> drank vodka till late
> and ate honeycd sweets.
> The rook cawed and praised
> this ghostly world,
> and the giant cuirassier
> drove along on his sledge.

Unlike many of her contemporaries, Akhmatova, wary of sudden shifts and radical transformations of style, was attracted by traditional forms, by the clarity, precision and harmony of the language of Pushkin and Baratynsky.† Today she still tends to poetic reminiscences, which at times have the effect of parallel mirrors deepening the perspective of the poem while bringing distant objects closer together ('The future matures in the past whose embers glow in the future . . .'). Literary names and associations, epigraphs, dedications, meetings

*Tsarskoe Selo, a country palace built for Catherine the Great and surrounded by country houses; also a small town where Akhmatova often stayed.
†Yevgeny Baratynsky (1800–1844), lyrical and philosophical poet, author of 'Edens', 'Feasts', 'Dance', etc.

and partings with the past ('As though I said goodbye
again to what I said goodbye to long ago . . .'), the
settling of accounts with herself and her memory – all
this, so far from hindering her, lightens her task: to
create, within the compass of a brief text, a sense of
space and freely move about in it, calling out to other
times and other spheres of being, communicating with
them and recording their voices. So wide is the space that
it can hold the universe, and if the communication is
in whispers or in silence, this no longer matters. Silence
in her verse is not a sign of solitude but of a presence of
ineffable majesty.

> You and I are a mountain of grief . . .
> you and I will never meet.
> Only try at midnight to send me
> a greeting through the stars.

The new quality in Akhmatova's work compels us
to look back and revise the conventional estimate of her
early work. Did she, even in that first, muted period of
her development, have in her as a hidden potential
what later, matured and rejuvenated, was to become
her strength?

Akhmatova was always recognized as a master of the
poetic self-portrait – a portrait so alive, alike and natural
in gesture and expression that it almost leapt out of the
framework of the poem. The small format proved
astonishingly capacious. Akhmatova had the gift of
putting a whole human life, with all its mysteries, its
psychological twists, into a single quatrain.

> I am happy. But what I hold most dear
> are the sloping forest path,

the simple crooked bridge,
and that there are only a few days left to wait.

If her early poems are packed with meaning and
images, equally striking at times are the range of her
intonations and the power of her voice – a voice of
which Mandelshtam once said, in a poem he dedicated
to her, that it could 'unshackle the soul'. Such are the
scope, the depth of feeling and tone that, in spite of the
muted orchestration, they reveal a character of vast,
massive, almost monumental stature. Everyone remem-
bers her lines:

> Then be accursed. I will not touch
> your damned soul with a groan or a glance.
> But I swear to you by the garden of the angels,
> I swear by the miracle-working ikon,
> and by the fire and smoke of our nights
> that I will never return.

They are more than is usually assumed – the outcry
of a hurt, humiliated and indignant woman: beyond the
shrill tirade of the woman is the artist, the scope of
whose personality it reveals.

Equally early Akhmatova showed her talent for
civic and patriotic verse. A striking example is a poem
written in 1917 as a rebuke to those who were about to
leave the country at the moment when the revolution
had set it ablaze. In the circumstances (though they are
presented in a gloomy enough light) what is significant
is the choice made by Akhmatova in favour of her own
country. According to Kornei Chukovsky, Aleksandr
Blok who loved this poem and knew it off by heart
considered it important on grounds of principle.

'Akhmatova is right,' he says, 'these are shameful words.
To run away from the Russian revolution is a disgrace.'

> I heard a voice. It called me consolingly,
> 'Come here, leave
> your god-forsaken country,
> abandon Russia forever.
> I'll wash the blood from your hands,
> and rip black shame from your heart,
> and give you a new name to cover
> the pain of defeat and humiliation.'
> But I quite calmly
> put my hands over my ears,
> that my grieving soul
> should not be defiled by these shameful words.

From the barest whisper to fiery eloquence, from downcast eyes to lightning and thunderbolts – such is the range of Akhmatova's inspiration and voice. This, it seems, is what later developed and gave her strength to follow a new course, wide enough for anything from patriotic oratory to the silence of lofty metaphysical meditation, and the arguing voices of the living and the dead.

Novy Mir, *No. 6, pp. 174–6, 1964.*   A. SINYAVSKY

from Evening

The door is half open,
the lime trees wave sweetly . . .
On the table, forgotten –
a whip and a glove.

The lamp casts a yellow circle . . .
I listen to the rustling.
Why did you go?
I don't understand . . .

Tomorrow the morning
will be clear and happy.
This life is beautiful,
heart, be wise;

You are utterly tired,
you beat calmer, duller . . .
You know, I read
that souls are immortal.   1911*

*Dates without parentheses are dates of composition; those in
parentheses indicate first publication.

The memory of the sun weakens in the heart,
the grass is more yellow,
the wind flutters the early snow-flakes
gently, gently.

No flow now in the narrow channels,
water freezes,
nothing will ever happen here,
ever!

In the empty sky the willow spread
a transparent fan.
Perhaps it's better that I did not become
your wife.

The memory of the sun weakens in the heart.
What is this? Darkness?
Perhaps! Within a night it will be
winter.   1911

20

The Grey-eyed King

Glory to you unrelenting pain!
Yesterday the grey-eyed king died.

The autumn night was stifling and crimson,
my husband on returning said calmly:

'You know they carried him from the hunt,
they found the body by the old oak.

Poor queen. He was so young!
In one night she turned grey.'

He found his pipe on the fireplace
and went off to his night work.

I will wake my little daughter now,
and look into her little grey eyes.

Outside the window the poplars rustle:
'Your king is on this earth no more.'   1910

The boy who plays the bagpipes,
the girl who weaves her wreath,
two paths crossed in the forest,
a small distant fire in the distant field.

I see everything. I retain everything,
lovingly, tenderly I cherish it in my heart.
Just one thing I never know
and cannot even remember any more.

I do not ask for wisdom or strength,
no, just let me warm myself by the fire!
I feel cold . . . Winged or wingless
no joyful god visits me.   1911

Today they brought no letter for me:
he forgot to write or maybe went away;
spring like a trill of silver laughter,
in the bay the ships rock.
Today they brought no letter for me . . .

He was with me such a short time ago,
so in love, tender, mine,
but that was in white winter,
now it's spring, and spring's melancholy is poison,
he was with me such a short time ago.

I hear: a light, trembling fiddle-bow
is beating, beating like agony before death,
and I fear my heart will burst.
I will not finish these tender lines . . .

In the Forest

Four diamonds – four eyes –
two of the owl and two of mine.
Terrible the end of the tale,
how my bridegroom died.

I lie on the thick, moist grass,
my words ring senselessly,
looking down self-importantly
the owl listens keenly to them.

Fir trees crowd close round us,
over us the sky – a black square;
you know, you know they killed him,
my elder brother killed him –

Not in a bloody duel,
not on the battlefield, not in war,
but on the deserted forest path,
when my lover was coming to me.   (1911)

from Rosary

To M. Lozinsky

It drags on without end, this heavy amber day.
Impossible the sadness, vain the waiting!
Once more the deer speaks of the Northern Lights –
its silvered voice sounds in the deer park.
I believed that there was cool snow,
and a blue font for the sick and needy,
and a jolting ride on a small sledge
with the ancient chimes of distant bells.   1912

I taught myself to live simply and wisely,
to look at the sky and pray to God,
and to wander long before evening
to tire my useless sadness.

When the burdocks rustle in the ravine
and the yellow-red rowanberry cluster droops
I write down happy verses
about life's decay, decay and beauty.

I come back. The fluffy cat
licks my palm, purrs so sweetly,
and the fire flares bright
on the saw-mill turret by the lake.

Only the cry of a stork landing on the roof
occasionally breaks the silence.
If you knock on my door
I may not even hear.   1912

In the Evening

There was such inexpressible sorrow
in the music in the garden.
The oysters in ice on the dish
smelt fresh and sharp of the sea.

He said to me 'I am a true friend!'
He touched my dress.
There is no passion
in the touch of his hands.

This is how one strokes a cat or a bird,
this is how one looks at a shapely horseback rider.
Only the laughter in his eyes
under the light gold of his eyelashes.

The violins' mourning voices
sing above the spreading smoke:
'Give thanks to heaven:
you are alone with your love for the first time.'

1913

I know, I know, again the skis
will creak drily.
A ruddy moon in the blue sky,
the sweetly sloping meadow.

In the palace the windows burn
cut off by silence.
Not a track, not a path,
only the ice-holes are dark.

Willow, tree of the water nymphs,
do not bar my way!
In the snowy twigs black jackdaws,
black jackdaws shelter.   1913

The Guest

Everything as before: blown snow
beats against the dining-room windows.
I have not changed,
but a man came to me.

I asked, 'What do you want?'
He said 'To be with you in hell.'
I laughed, 'No doubt you'll
ruin us both.'

But he lifted his thin hand
and softly touched the flowers:
'Tell me how they kiss you,
tell me how you kiss.'

His dull eyes looked
fixedly at my ring.
Not a single muscle moved
in his radiant, evil face.

Oh, I know: it is his delight
to know intensely and passionately,
that he needs nothing,
that I can refuse him nothing.   January 1914

To Aleksandr Blok

I visited the poet.
Midday, Sunday.
It was quiet in the big room
and a frost outside the window,

and a crimson sun
above the shaggy dove-grey smoke . . .
The silent host
looks at me piercingly.

He has eyes which everyone
always remembers.
Better for me to be careful
and not look into them at all.

But I remember a conversation,
a smoky midday, Sunday
in a high, grey house
by the sea-gates of the Neva.   1914

from White Flock

Blue varnish faded in the sky,
the song of the ocarina swells.
It is only a clay pipe,
no reason to complain about it like that.
Who told it my sins,
and why does it forgive me? . . .
Through the tousled foliage of the alder
the sun floods the earth with slanting light.   1912

Black road twisted.
Rain drizzled.
Somebody asked me
to go with him a little way.
I agreed, but forgot
to look at him.
Later it was so strange
remembering that road.
The mist floated like the incense
of a thousand censers.
My companion obstinately
vexed my soul with his song.
I remember the dark gates
and the end of the road,
and there the man who walked with me
whispered: 'Forgive . . .'
He gave me an ancient crucifix,
as though he were my dear brother.
All around I hear the melody
of a song of the steppe.
I am at home, and not at home.
I cry and am sad . . .
Answer me, stranger,
I am looking for you.   (1913)

I see, I see the crescent moon
through thick broom foliage.
I hear, hear the regular beat
of unshod hooves.

What? You too don't want to sleep,
in a year you couldn't forget me,
not used to finding
your bed empty?

Don't I talk with you
in the falcons' sharp cry?
Don't I look into your eyes
from the dull, white pages?

Why do you circle, like a thief,
round the silent house?
Or do you remember the agreement
and wait for me alive?

I am falling asleep. The moon has thrown
its blade into the stifling dark.
Again hoof beats. It is my warm
heart that beats so.   (1914)

Parting

Evening, sloping
path before me.
Only yesterday, in love –
he implored, 'Don't forget.'
Now only the winds
and the cries of the shepherds.
The cedars in uproar
by the clean springs.   1914

The road by the shore garden looms dark.
The lamps are yellow and fresh.
I am very calm. Only do not
talk to me about him.
You are sweet and true – we will be friends . . .
Walk around, kiss, grow old . . .
And light months will fly past
like the snowy stars above us.   1914

Frosty sun. From the parade
the troops are marching, marching.
I am happy with the January midday,
my worries are few.

Here I remember every twig
and every silhouette.
Crimson light drops
through the frost's white net.

Here the house was all but white,
glass-porched.
So many times my deathly pale hand
held the bell-ring.

So many times . . . Play on, soldiers,
and I will seek my house;
I will recognize it by the sloping roof,
by the eternal ivy.

But someone moved it away
carried it off to other towns,
or excised from the mind
for ever the road that led there . . .

In the distance the bagpipes die away,
snow flies like cherry blossom . . .
and it is obvious nobody knows
that there is no white house.   1914

'Tall woman, where is your gipsy boy,
who cried under the black shawl,
where is your small first-born,
what news of him, what memory?'

'A mother's fate is a torture of joy,
I was not worthy of it.
They unlocked the wicket gate into white paradise,
Mary Magdalene took my little son.

My every day is happy and good,
I lost myself in the long spring.
Yet still my arms mourn for their burden,
yet still I hear his crying in my sleep.

My heart becomes uneasy, weary,
and then I remember nothing,
but constantly walk the dark rooms,
but constantly search for his cradle.'   1914

How can you look at the Neva,
how can you go out on the bridges?
Not for nothing have I been called sad
since I first dreamed of you.
The wings of black angels are sharp,
the last judgement is near
and the crimson bonfires
like roses flower in the snow.   1914

He was jealous, worried and tender,
like God's sun he loved me.
He killed my white bird
to stop it singing of the past.

Coming into the room at sunset, he said:
'Love me, laugh, write poetry!'
I buried the happy bird
beyond the round well near the old alder tree.

I promised him not to cry.
But my heart turned to stone,
and it seems that always, and everywhere
I will hear its sweet voice.   1914

To N. G. Chulkova

These days come before spring:
the meadow rests under thick snow,
the dry trees rustle gaily,
the warm wind soft and resilient.
The body marvels at its lightness,
you do not recognize your house,
and the song that annoyed you before,
enraptured, you sing as new.   1915

Dream

I knew you were dreaming of me,
that's why I couldn't get to sleep.
The murky lamp hazed blue
and showed me the road.

You saw the Tsaritsa's garden,*
the intricate white palace,
the black tracery of the fences
by the echoing stone steps.

You walked, not knowing the way,
and thought, 'Quicker, quicker.
If only I could find her.
I must not wake before I meet her.'

The sentry by the great gates
called out: 'Where are you going?'
The ice crackled and broke,
water blackened under foot.

This lake – you thought –
there is a little island in the lake . . .
Suddenly a blue flame
gleamed out of the darkness.

*'. . . the Tsaritsa's garden': this poem is probably set in the
park in Tsarskoe Selo, outside Leningrad, which is a recurring
motif in Akhmatova's work. The New Garden and the English
Garden formed the Yekaterinsky Sad – that is the 'Tsaritsa's
garden', which was on one side of the palace. The gardens
were laid out around 1720 and there is a small lake in the park.

In the harsh light of naked day
you woke up and groaned,
and for the first time
loudly called me by my name.   1915

I still see hilly Pavlovsk,*
the round meadow, the lifeless water,
very languid and very shadowy.
I will never forget it.

As you enter through the iron gates
a blissful shudder touches your body,
you do not live, but rejoice and rave,
or live completely differently.

In the late autumn the wind wanders
fresh and sharp, happy in the wilderness.
In white frost black firs
stand on thawing snow.

Filled with the flames of delirium,
the sweet voice sounds like a song,
and on the Citharode's bronze shoulder
a red-breasted bird sits.   1915

* 'Pavlovsk', like Tsarskoe Selo, is outside Leningrad and has a
palace (built 1782-6) and a fine park with statuary.

'Coorlee, coorlee!' The others call
the wounded crane
when the autumn fields
are crumbly and warm.

And I, ill, hear the calls,
the noise of golden wings
out of the thick, low cloud
and the dense brushwood.

'It's time to fly, to fly
over field and river.
No longer can you sing
and wipe tears from your cheek
with a feeble hand.'   1915

You cannot get here
by boat or by cart.
Deep water
lies on rotten snow.
Farmstead already besieged
on all sides.
That same Robinson
pines away near by,
goes to look at the sledge,
at the skis, the horses,
and, later, sits
on the sofa, waits for me,
rips the rug in half
with his short spur.
The mirrors no longer see
his gentle smile.   1916

Like a white stone in the well's depth
one memory lies within me.
I can't and don't want to fight it:
it is happiness and it is suffering.

It seems to me that he who looks closely
into my eyes will see it immediately.
He will become sadder and more pensive
than someone listening to a shameful tale.

I know that the gods metamorphosed
men into objects and did not kill consciousness.
So that the marvel of sorrow may live for ever,
you are metamorphosed into my memory.   1916

The town vanished. Almost alive,
the window of the last house looked out.
This place is completely unfamiliar,
smell of burning and darkness in the fields.

But when the faltering moon
cut the storm curtain
we saw: up the hill, towards the forest
a lame man made his way.

It was terrible, that he outran
the troika – well-fed, eager horses –
stopped for a while and again hobbled
under his heavy burden.

We hardly managed to notice
when he appeared by our kibitka,*
his blue eyes gleamed like stars
lighting his exhausted face.

I held out the baby to him,
he lifted his fetter-marked hand
and clearly uttered this blessing:
'Your son will live and be healthy.'   1916

* Russian hooded sledge.

Everything promised him to me:
the sky's faded, scarlet rim,
sweet dream on Christmas Eve,
the many-sounding wind at Easter,

the red vine shoots,
waterfalls in the park,
two large dragonflies
on the rusty iron fence.

I could not but believe
that he would be friends with me,
as I walked the hill slopes
on the hot stone path.   1916

It seems that man's voice
will never ring out here,
only the stone-age wind
beats on the black gates.
It seems to me that I alone
survived under the sky,
because I was the first who wished
to drink death's wine.   1917

from Plantain

I don't speak with anyone for a week.
I just sit on a stone by the sea.
It pleases me that the green waves' spray
is salt like my tears.
Springs and winters passed, but somehow
I only remembered one spring.
The nights became warmer, the snow began to thaw.
I went out to look at the moon.
Meeting me alone in the young pines
a stranger asked me quietly:
'Are you the one I searched for everywhere,
for whom since my earliest days
I have been glad and grieved – as though for a dear
    sister?'
I answered the stranger, 'No!'
And when the light from the heavens shone on his face
I gave him my hands.
He gave me a secret ring
to guard me against love.
And he told me four landmarks
where we must meet again:
the sea, the curving bay, the high lighthouse,
and – most important – the wormwood . . .
Let my life end as it began,
I have told what I know: Amen!   1916

Along the firm crest of the snowdrift
to my white, mysterious house,
both of us so quiet now,
we are walking in tender silence.
And sweetest of all songs ever sung
is to me this fulfilled dream,
the rocking of brushed twigs
and the slight sound of your spurs. January 1917

To wake up at dawn
from joy's stranglehold
and look through the cabin window
at the green waves,
or on deck in foul weather
wrapped in a fluffy coat
listen to the engine's beat.
Not to think about anything,
but sensing the meeting
with him, who has become my star,
and grow younger each hour
from the salt spray and wind.   1917

For a whole day, fearing its own groans,
the crowd tosses in death's anguish.
Over the river on funeral banners
malevolent skulls laugh.
This is why I sang and dreamt,
they split my heart in two,
with the sudden quiet after the salvo
death sent patrols from yard to yard.   1917

I asked the cuckoo
how many years I would live . . .
The pine tops trembled,
a yellow shaft fell to the grass.
No sound in the fresh forest depth . . .
I am going home,
and the cool wind caresses
my hot brow.   1919

from Anno Domini

Little Song

I used to keep quiet from morning
about my dream's song to me.
For the flushed rose and for the sun's ray
and for me there is one fate.
Snow slides from the sloping hills,
I am whiter than snow,
but I dream sweetly of the banks
of flooding, turbid rivers.
The fresh murmur of the fir thicket
is more peaceful than dawn meditations.   1916

A log bridge blackened and twisted.
The burdocks stand as high as a man.
The thick nettle forests sing that
the scythe will not flash through them.
In the evening over the lake a sigh is heard,
rough moss has crawled over the walls.

There I was
twenty-one.
The black, stifling honey
was sweet to the lips.

The twigs tore
my white silk dress,
the nightingale sang unceasingly
on the crooked pine.

At a given call
he came out of hiding,
like a wild wood-spirit,
but more tender than a sister.

Run over the plain,
swim across the river,
then afterwards,
I will not say leave me.   1917

To fall ill as one should, to meet
everyone again in a blazing delirium.
To walk down broad avenues
in the sunny wind-filled seashore garden.

Now even the dead and the exiles
agree to come into my house.
Lead the child to me by the hand,
I have missed him for so long.

I will eat blue grapes with my darlings,
I will drink iced wine,
and watch the grey waterfall stream over
on to the damp, flint bed.   1922

The freak autumn built a high vault in the sky,
the clouds were ordered not to darken the vault.
The people marvelled: September is passing
and where are the chill, damp days?
The murky canal waters turned emerald,
the nettles smelled like roses, only stronger.
The air was sultry with sunsets, unbearable, devilish,
    crimson,
we will all remember them till the end of our days.
The sun was like a rebel forcing the capital,
and the spring-like autumn caressed it so thirstily
that it seemed the transparent snowdrop would
    blossom white . . .
That was when you, cool and calm, came to my door.

                                                    1922

It is good here: rustle and snow-crunch,
frost fiercer every morning,
a bush of blinding ice roses
bows in white flame.
On the splendid finery of the snow
a ski-track – memory
that long ages ago
we passed here together.   1922

New Year Ballad

The moon, weary in the pall of cloud,
cast a murky glance at the hill.
The table was laid for six,
and only one place was empty.

My husband, myself and my friends
are seeing the new year in.
Why are my fingers covered as with blood?
Why does the wine burn like poison?

The host with full glass raised
was impressive – immobile.
'I drink to the earth of our own forest glades,
in which we all lie.'

A friend looked at my face,
suddenly remembered God knows what,
and exclaimed: 'I drink to her songs
in which we all live!'

But a third, not understanding,
as he went out into the dark,
answering my thoughts
said: 'We ought to drink to him
who is not with us yet.'   1923

By the Sea Shore*

I

The bays broke up the low shore,
all the sails had run off to the sea,
and I used to dry my salt-crusted hair
a couple of miles from land on a flat rock.
A green fish swam to me,
a white seagull flew to me.
I was daring, evil and happy,
and had no idea that this was happiness.
I buried my check dress in the sand
lest the wind should blow it away, or a tramp
carry it off, and I swam far out to sea
and lay on the dark, warm waves.
As I returned, from the east
the lighthouse already beamed its alternating light.
A monk at the gates of the Chersonese
said: 'Why are you wandering at night?'
The natives knew – I divine water,
and if they were digging a new well
they called me to find the spot
and save the men wasted work.
I used to gather French bullets,
like one gathers mushrooms or bilberries,
and brought home in my skirt
the rusted splinters of heavy shells,
and I spoke crossly to my sister:

*See note on p. 106.

61

'When I become empress
I will build six battleships
and six gunboats,
to protect my bays
right down to Cape Fiolent.'
And in the evening I prayed
by my bed to the dark ikon
that the hail would not beat down the cherries,
that the fat fish would be caught,
and that the crafty tramp
would not notice the check dress.

I used to be friends with the fishermen,
and when the rain pelted down I often sat
with them under an upturned boat.
I heard about the sea, and remembered,
secretly believing every word.
The fishermen became used to me.
If I was not on the quay
the old one sent the girl for me,
and she shouted: 'Our men are back!
Now we can fry the flatfish.'

The tall boy was grey-eyed,
half a year younger than me.
He brought me white roses,
white muscat roses,
and asked gently: 'Can I
sit with you on the rocks?'
I laughed, 'Why do I need roses
with their sharp thorns?' He asked,
'What can I do then,

if I am so in love with you?'
I got annoyed: 'Stupid!
What are you?' I asked, 'A prince?'
This was the grey-eyed boy,
half a year younger than me.
'I want to marry you,'
he said, 'soon I will be grown up
and will go with you to the north . . .'
The tall boy cried
because I did not want the roses,
did not want to go to the north.
I comforted him badly:
'Think, I will be empress,
why should I need such a husband?'
'Well then, I will become a monk,'
he said, 'near to you in the Chersonese.'
'No, don't bother. The only thing
monks do is die.
If you go there they are always burying someone –
and the others don't mourn him.'
The boy went away without a farewell.
He took the muscat roses
and I let him go.
I did not say 'Stay with me.'
The secret parting pain
cried out like a white seagull
over the grey, wormwood steppe,
over desert, dead Korsun.

2

The bays broke up the low shore,
a smoky sun fell into the sea.

The gipsy woman came out of her cave,
beckoned me to her with her finger:
'My beauty, why do you walk around barefoot?
Soon you will be happy and rich.
Expect a noble guest before Easter,
you will greet the noble guest;
not with your beauty, not with your love,
but with your song alone will you entice the guest.'
I gave the gipsy a little chain
and a small gold christening cross.
I thought joyfully: 'Look, my darling
has given me the first news of himself.'
But out of anxiety I stopped
loving all my bays and caves.
I did not scare the viper in the reeds,
I did not bring crabs for supper,
I used to walk along the gully to the south
beyond the vineyard to the stone quarry –
it wasn't a short way.
It often happened that the owner
of the new farm waved to me,
called me from afar: 'Why don't you ever come in?
Everybody says you bring good luck.'
I would answer: 'Only horseshoes,
and the new moon that looks
into your eyes from the right are bringers of luck.'
I did not like to go indoors.
Dry winds blew from the east,
large stars fell from the sky,
in the lower church services were held
for the sailors who had gone out to sea;
jellyfish floated into the bay,

like stars fallen during the night
they gleamed blue deep underwater.
How the cranes called 'Coorlee' in the sky,
how the cicadas chattered restlessly,
how the soldier's wife sang of sorrow,
my keen ear remembered it all.
Only I knew no song
to make my prince stay with me.
I began to dream often of a girl
wearing thin bracelets and a short dress,
with a white reed-pipe in her cool hands.
She sits calmly, looks long,
will not ask about my sorrow,
and will not speak of her sorrow
only tenderly strokes my shoulder.
How will the prince recognize me?
Surely he remembers my features?
Who will point him out our old house?
Our house is well off the road.

Autumn changed to rainy winter,
wind blew through the window in the white room,
ivy hung on the low garden wall.
Strange dogs came to the yard,
howled under my window till dawn.
It was a hard time for the heart.
I whispered as I looked at the door:
'Oh God, we will rule wisely,
and build great churches by the sea,
and tall lighthouses.
We will take care of water and land,
we will not hurt a soul.'

3

The dark sea suddenly became kinder,
the swallows returned to their nests,
and the earth turned red with poppies,
and it was good again by the sea-shore.
Summer came in one night –
so we did not even glimpse spring.
I was no longer afraid
that my new fate might never come.
On the evening of Palm Sunday
as I came out of church I said to my sister:
'For you, my candle and my rosary,
our Bible I leave at home,
Easter will be here in a week,
it is high time that I got ready –
no doubt the prince is on his way by now,
he will come for me by sea.'
My sister wondered at my words in silence,
just sighed, no doubt remembered
the words of the gipsy by the cave,
'Will he bring you a necklace,
and rings set with blue stones?'
'No' I said, 'We do not know what
gift he is preparing for me.'
I was the same age as my sister,
and we were so alike
that when we were small our mother
could only recognize us by our birthmarks.
My sister could not walk from childhood,
she lay like a wax doll;
she was never cross with anyone

and she used to embroider a holy cloth.
Even in her sleep, she raved on about her work:
I heard her whispering:
'The Virgin's cloak will be blue,
o God, I can't find any pearls
for John the Apostle's tears.'
The small yard was overgrown with goose-grass and
     mint,
the little donkey nibbled the grass by the wicket gate,
on a long wicker armchair
lay Lena with her arms outstretched,
always worrying about her work –
on such a holiday it is a sin to work.
The salt wind from the Chersonese
brought us the Easter bells,
each blow echoed in my heart,
coursed with my blood through the veins.
'Lena, darling Lena,' I said to my sister,
'I am going to the shore now.
If the prince comes for me
show him the way.
Let him catch me up in the steppe:
today I want to go down to the sea.'
'Where did you hear the song,
the song which will entice the prince?'
My sister asked with half-opened eyes,
'You don't even go into the town,
and here they don't sing such songs.'
I bent close up to her ear
and whispered, 'I'll tell you, Lena,
I thought up the song myself,
it's the best song in the world.'

She did not believe me, and long,
long, she kept reproachfully silent.

4

The sun lay at the bottom of the well,
scolopendras basked on the stones,
and tumble-weed ran riot
like a hunchback clown cavorting,
and the high-soaring sky
was blue like the Virgin's cloak –
it was never like this before.
From midday light sailing ships chased each other,
many lazy white sails crowded
round Constantine's battery –
wind obviously favourable now.
I walked slowly along the bay to the cape,
to the black, shattered, sharp cliffs
foam-covered when the surf comes in,
and repeated my new song.
I knew: whoever the prince is with
he will hear my voice and be moved.
So, like a gift from God,
each word was dear to me.
The first boat did not sail, it flew,
and the second caught it up
while the others were hardly visible.
I don't remember how I lay by the water,
I don't know how I dozed off then.
Suddenly I woke: I saw a sail
flapping nearby. In front of me
a huge old man standing up to his waist
in the clear water, scrabbles his hands

in the deep cracks of the shore cliffs,
hoarse-voiced calls for help.
Loudly I began to repeat the prayer
I was taught when young
to ward off terror from my dreams,
to ward off evil from our house.
Only I spoke: 'You are the Saviour!'
I looked – something showed white in the old man's
    arms –
my heart froze.
The sailor had carried out the man who sailed
the most joyful and winged sailing ship,
and placed him on the dark rocks.

For a long time I did not dare trust myself,
I bit my fingers to wake up:
my beautiful, tender prince
lay quietly and looked at the sky.
Those eyes, greener than the sea,
darker than our cypresses,
I saw them fade . . .
Better for me to have been born blind.
He groaned and shouted inarticulately:
'Swallow, o swallow. What agony!'
Perhaps he saw me as a bird.

I returned home at dusk.
It was quiet in the dark room.
A thin, tiny crimson flame
stood high over the ikon lamp.
'The prince did not come for you,'
Lena said when she heard footsteps.

'I waited for him till vespers,
and sent the children down to the harbour.'

'He will never come for me,
he will never return, Lena,
my prince died today.'
My sister crossed herself again and again.
She turned her face to the wall and was silent.
In my heart I knew Lena was crying.

I heard that they sang for the prince:
'Christ is risen from the dead' –
and the round church
shone with an ineffable light.   1914

from Reed

If the moon's horror splashes,
the whole town dissolves in poison.
Without the slightest hope of going to sleep
I see through the green murk
not my childhood, not the sea,
nor the butterflies' wedding flight
over the bed of snow-white narcissi,
in that sixteenth year . . .
but the eternally petrified round dance
of the cypresses over your grave.   1928

71

Boris Pasternak*

He who compared himself to a horse's eye
squints, looks, sees, recognizes,
and already the puddles shine
in a diamond fusion, the ice pines away.

The backyards rest in a lilac haze,
platforms, logs, leaves, clouds.
The engine's whistle, the crunch of melon peel,
a timid hand in a fragrant kid glove.

He rings, thunders, gnashes, beats in the breakers –
and is suddenly quiet, this means
he is treading the pine needles, fearful lest
he should scare awake the light dream-sleep of space.

And this means that he is counting the grains
in the empty ears, this means
he has come again from some funeral
to the cursed, black, Daryal* tombstone.

Moscow tedium burns again,
death's sleigh bells ring in the distance –
Who has got lost two steps from home,
where the snow is waist deep and an end to all?

Because he compared smoke with Laocoon,*
sang of the graveyard thistle,
because he filled the earth with a new sound
in a new space of mirrored stanzas,

*See note on p. 106.

he is rewarded with a form of eternal childhood,
with the bounty and vigilance of the stars,
the whole world was his inheritance
and he shared it with everyone.   19 January 1936

When a man dies
his portraits change.
His eyes look in a different way,
his lips smile a different smile.
I noticed this on returning
from the funeral of a poet.
Since then I have often checked it,
and my theory has been confirmed.　　　　1940

Willow

I grew in patterned silence
in the cool nursery of a young age.
Man's voice held no sweetness for me
but I understood the wind.
I loved the burdocks and the nettles
but above all the silver willow.
Thankful it lived with me
all its life, weeping branches
fanning sleeplessness with dreams.
Strange – I outlived it.
A stump grows there now, other voices
of other willows say something
under our unchanging heavens.
I am silent . . . as though my brother were dead.

1940

from Seventh Book

Three Autumns

For me the summer smiles are simply indistinct,
I find no secrets in winter,
but I could pick out unerringly
three autumns in each year.

The first a holiday chaos
spiting yesterday's summer.
Leaves fly like notebook scraps,
smoke smells sweet as incense,
everything moist, gay and bright.

First the birches start the dance
throwing on their transparent attire,
hastily shaking off their fleeting tears
on their neighbour over the fence.

But it happens . . . the tale is scarce begun . . .
a second, a minute – and look,
the second one comes, passionless like conscience,
sombre as an air raid.

Everything suddenly seems paler, older.
Summer's comfort is plundered,
far-off marches played on gold trumpets
float over the scented fog . . .

The sky vault is closed
in cold waves of incense
but the wind started blowing, all was swept open, and
   immediately
everyone understood: the play is ending,
this is not the third autumn but death.   1943

Asia, your lynx eyes
spied something out in me,
teased out something hidden,
born of silence,
difficult and tormenting
like the midday heat at Termezsk.
As though all former memory flowed
into the conscience like scorching lava.
As though the tears I wept myself
I drank from another's cupped hands.   1945

Tashkent Breaks into Blossom

As if somebody ordered it
the city suddenly became bright –
it came into every court
in a white, light apparition.
Their breathing is more understandable than words,
in the burning blue sky
their reflection is doomed
to lie at the bottom of the ditch.

I will remember the roof of stars
in the radiance of eternal glory,
and the small rolls of bread
in the young hands
of dark-haired mothers.   1944

From *the Cycle of Tashkent Pages*

That night we both went out of our minds,
only an ominous darkness lit our way,
the ditches muttered,
carnations smelt of Asia.

We passed through a strange town,
through a smoky song and midnight heat:
alone under the constellation of the Snake
not daring to look at each other.

This could be Baghdad or Stamboul
but alas, not Warsaw, not Leningrad,
and this bitter anomaly was
suffocating like the smell of an orphanage.

It seemed ages march side by side,
an invisible hand banged a tambourine.
Sounds like secret signs
circled before us in the dark.

I was with you in the mysterious haze
as though we were walking in no-man's land,
but the moon like a diamond felucca
suddenly sailed out over our meeting-parting . . .

And if that night comes back to you,
in your fate which is a mystery to me,
know that this sacred moment
was somebody's dream.   1959

Fragment

... And it seemed that these were fires
flying with me until dawn,
and I did not find out
what colour were these strange eyes.

And everything around trembled and sang,
and I did not find out if you were friend or foe,
if this was winter or summer. 1959

Don't frighten me with threats of fate
and the great boredom of the North,
this is my first holiday with you,
they call this holiday – parting.
Never mind that we won't meet the dawn,
that the moon did not roam above us,
today I will give you
gifts unheard of in this world:
my reflection in the water
in the hour when the evening stream does not sleep,
the look that did not help
the falling star to return to the heavens.
The echo of a tired, cracked voice
which once was fresh and summery –
so that you could hear without shuddering
the gossip of the crows round Moscow,
so that the damp of an October day
became sweeter than the softness of May.
Remember me, my angel,
remember me, at least till the first snow.

October 1959

Death of Sophocles

Then the king learnt that Sophocles was dead (Legend)

That night an eagle flew from the heavens to
   Sophocles' house,
and dismally the choir of cicadas suddenly rang out
   from the garden.
At that hour the genius was already passing into
   immortality,
skirting the enemy camp by the walls of his native
   town.
And this was when the king had a strange dream:
Dionysus himself ordered him to raise the siege,
so as not to let the noise disturb the burial-rites,
and allow the Athenians the joy of honouring him.

1961

Alexander at Thebes

The young king must have been terrible and menacing
as he pronounced: 'You will destroy Thebes.'
And the old leader beheld that proud city,
as he had known it once of old.
Put it all, all to the fire. And the king counted
the towers, the gates, the temples – a wonder of the
    world,
but suddenly he paused, his face lit up and he said:
'Only make sure that the house of the Poet is not
    touched.'   1961

On the Road

A land not our own
and yet eternally memorable,
and in the sea there is tender-iced
and unsalt water.

On the bottom – sand whiter than chalk,
and air as drunk as wine,
and the pink mass of the pines
laid bare in the sunset hour.

The sunset itself in the ethereal waves
is such that I cannot tell
if this is the end of the day or of the world,
or the secret of secrets is within me again.   1964

from *Northern Elegies*

2

So here it is, that autumn landscape
which I have feared so much all my life:
the sky like a flaming abyss,
the sounds of the town – like sounds
heard from the after-life and eternally alien.
As though everything which all my life
I fought inside me has taken on
a separate life and is incarnate in
these blind walls and this black garden . . .
And at that moment behind my shoulder
my old house was still following me
with a screwed up, malevolent eye,
with that unforgettable window.
Fifteen years – as though
they pretended to be fifteen granite ages.
But I myself was like granite;
now pray, torment yourself, call me
sea princess. It's all the same, let it go . . .
But I had to assure myself,
that this had all happened many times,
and not to me alone, but to others also –
and even worse. No, not worse – better.
And my voice – this really was
the most fearful thing – spoke out of the darkness:
'Fifteen years ago, with what song did you
meet the day? You begged the heavens,
the chorus of stars, the chorus of waters
to greet your solemn meeting
with him whom you left today . . .

So here is your silver wedding:
call the guests, make yourself beautiful, triumph!'

1943

4

Memories have three epochs.
And the first is like yesterday.
The soul is under their blessed vault,
and the body is in the bliss of their shadow.
Laughter has not died down and the tears stream,
the ink stain is unwiped on the table,
the kiss is imprinted on the heart,
unique, parting, unforgettable . . .
But this does not last for long . . .
The firmament is no longer overhead, and somewhere
in a dull suburb there is a lonely house,
where it's cold in winter and hot in summer,
where a spider lives and dust lies on everything,
where passionate letters burn to ash,
portraits change stealthily,
and people come to it as though to a grave,
and wash their hands when they get home,
and shake off a quick tear
from their tired lids, and sigh heavily . . .
But the clocks tick, one spring
replaces another, the sky turns pink,
names of towns change,
and eye-witnesses of events die,
and there is no one to cry with, no one to reminisce
    with.
Those shadows pass from us slowly
which we no longer call upon,
whose return would be terrible to us.
And once awake, we see that we have forgotten
the very road that led to the lonely house,

and choking with shame and anger,
we run to it, but (as in a dream)
everything is different there: people, things, walls,
and nobody knows us; we are strangers.
We got to the wrong place . . . Oh God!
Now comes the most bitter moment:
we realize that we could not contain
this past in the frontiers of our life,
and it is almost as alien to us
as to our neighbour in the flat,
and that we would not recognize those who have died,
and those whom God parted from us
got on splendidly without us –
even better . . .   1953

Requiem 1935-1940

No, not under the vault of another sky,
not under the shelter of other wings.
I was with my people then,
there where my people were doomed to be.   1961

Instead of a Foreword

During the terrible years of Yezhovshchina* I spent
seventeen months in the prison queues in Leningrad.
One day someone recognized me. Then a woman with
lips blue with cold who was standing behind me, and of
course had never heard of my name, came out of the
numbness which affected us all and whispered in my
ear – (we all spoke in whispers there):
   'Can you describe this?'
   I said, 'I can!'
   Then something resembling a smile slipped over what
had once been her face.
                                                1 April 1957
                                                Leningrad

*'Yezhovshchina': Yezhov was head of Stalin's secret police
in the late 1930s and was himself purged.

Dedication

The mountains bend before this grief,
the great river does not flow,
but the prison locks are strong
and behind them the convicts' holes,
and a deathly sadness.
For someone the fresh wind blows,
for someone the sunset basks . . .
We don't know, we are the same everywhere;
we only hear the repellent clank of keys,
the heavy steps of the soldiers.
We rose as though to early mass,
and went through the savage capital,
and we used to meet there, more lifeless than the dead,
the sun lower, the Neva mistier,
but in the distance hope still sings.
Condemned . . . Immediately the tears start,
one woman, already isolated from everyone else,
as though her life had been wrenched from her heart,
as though she had been smashed flat on her back,
still, she walks on . . . staggers . . . alone . . .
Where now are the chance friends
of my two hellish years?
What do they see in the Siberian blizzard,
what comes to them in the moon's circle?
I send them my farewell greeting.   March 1940

Introduction

It was a time when only the dead
smiled, happy in their peace.
And Leningrad dangled like a useless pendant
at the side of its prisons.
A time when, tortured out of their minds,
the convicted walked in regiments,
and the steam whistles sang
their short parting song.
Stars of death stood over us,
and innocent Russia squirmed*
under the bloody boots,
under the wheels of black Marias.

*'Russia': in the Russian – 'Rus', the traditional name for
Russia.

1*

They took you away at dawn,
I walked after you as though you were being borne
  out,
the children were crying in the dark room,
the candle swam by the ikon-stand.
The cold of the ikon on your lips.
Death sweat on your brow . . . Do not forget!
I will howl by the Kremlin towers
like the wives of the Streltsy.†   1935

2

The quiet Don flows quietly,
the yellow moon goes into the house,

goes in with its cap askew,
the yellow moon sees the shadow.

This woman is sick,
this woman is alone,

husband in the grave, son in prison,
pray for me.

3

No, this is not me – someone else suffers.
I couldn't stand this: let black drapes
cover what happened,
and let them take away the street lights . . .
   Night.

4

If I could show you, the mocker,
everybody's favourite,
happy sinner of Tsarskoe Selo,★
how your life will turn out:
you will stand at Kresty†
three hundredth in the line with your prison parcel,
and set fire to the new year ice
with your hot tears.
There the prison poplar sways,
silence – and how many
innocent lives are ending there . . .

★See note to p. 15.

†'Kresty': a prison built on the Vyborg side of Leningrad in
1893. It literally means 'Crosses' (referring to the layout of the
buildings) – and the additional sense of 'standing before the
cross' should be borne in mind; cf. parts 6 and 10.

5

For seventeen months I have been screaming,
calling you home.
I flung myself at the executioner's feet.
You are my son and my terror.
Everything is confused for ever,
and I can no longer tell
beast from man,
and how long I must wait for the execution.
Only the dusty flowers,
the clank of censers, and tracks
leading from somewhere to nowhere.
An enormous star
looks me straight in the eye
and threatens swift destruction.   1939

6

Weightless weeks fly by,
I will never grasp what happened.
How the white nights looked
at you, my son, in prison,
how they look again
with the burning eye of the hawk,
they speak of your tall cross,
they speak of death.   1939

7

Verdict

The stone word fell
on my still living breast.
Never mind, I was prepared,
somehow I'll come to terms with it.

Today I have much work to do:
I must finally kill my memory,
I must, so my soul can turn to stone,
I must learn to live again.

Or else . . . The hot summer rustle,
like holiday time outside my window.
I have felt this coming for a long time,
this bright day and the empty house.

Summer 1939

8

To Death

You will come anyway – so why not now?
I am waiting for you – it's very difficult for me.
I have put out the light and opened the door
to you, so simple and wonderful.
Assume any shape you like,
burst in as a poison gas shell,
or creep up like a burglar with a heavy weight,
or poison me with typhus vapours.
Or come with a denunciation thought up by you
and known *ad nauseam* to everyone,
so that I may see over the blue cap★
the janitor's fear-whitened face.
I don't care now. The Yenisey rolls on,†
the Pole star shines.
And the blue lustre of loving eyes
conceals the final horror.   19 August 1939

★'the blue cap' and 'the janitor' : an arrest.

†'Yenisey': river in Siberia where many of the concentration
camps were.

9

Already madness has covered
half my soul with its wing,
and gives me strong liquor to drink,
and lures me to the black valley.

I realized that I must
hand victory to it,
as I listened to my delirium,
already alien to me.

It will not allow me to take
anything away with me
(however I beseech it,
however I pester it with prayer):

not the terrible eyes of my son,
the rock-like suffering,
not the day when the storm came,
not the prison visiting hour,

nor the sweet coolness of hands,
nor the uproar of the lime trees' shadows,
nor the distant, light sound –
the comfort of last words.   4 May 1940

10

Crucifixion

'Weep not for Me, Mother,
in the grave I have life.'

I

The choir of angels glorified the great hour,
the heavens melted in flames.
He said to His Father: 'Why hast Thou forsaken Me?'
and to His Mother: 'Oh, weep not for Me . . .'

II

Mary Magdalene smote her breast and wept,
the disciple whom He loved turned to stone,
but where the Mother stood in silence
nobody even dared look.   1940–43

Epilogue

I found out how faces droop,
how terror looks out from under the eyelids,
how suffering carves on cheeks
hard pages of cuneiform,
how curls ash-blonde and black
turn silver overnight,
a smile fades on submissive lips,
fear trembles in a dry laugh.
I pray not for myself alone,
but for everyone who stood with me,
in the cruel cold, in the July heat,
under the blind, red wall.

11

The hour of remembrance has drawn close again.
I see you, hear you, feel you.

The one they hardly dragged to the window,
the one who no longer treads this earth,

the one who shook her beautiful head,
and said: 'Coming here is like coming home.'

I would like to call them all by name,
but the list was taken away and I can't remember.

For them I have woven a wide shroud
from the humble words I heard among them.

I remember them always, everywhere,
I will never forget them, whatever comes.

And if they gag my tormented mouth
with which one hundred million people cry,

then let them also remember me
on the eve of my remembrance day.

If they ever think of building
a memorial to me in this country,

I solemnly give my consent,
only with this condition: not to build it

near the sea where I was born;
my last tie with the sea is broken;

nor in Tsarsky Sad by the hallowed stump
where an inconsolable shadow seeks me,

but here, where I stood three hundred hours,
and they never unbolted the door for me.

Since even in blessed death I am terrified
that I will forget the thundering of the Black Marias,

forget how the hateful door slammed,
how an old woman howled like a wounded beast.

And let the melting snow stream
like tears from my motionless, bronze eyelids,

let the prison dove call in the distance
and the boats go quietly on the Neva.

March 1940

Notes

Page 61:

By the Sea Shore   In 'Briefly about Myself', which preceded
the 1961 edition of her poems, Akhmatova wrote about her
youth: 'I spent each summer near Sevastopol on the shores of
Streletskaya bay, and there I made friends with the sea. The
most striking impression of these years was the ancient Cher-
sonese near which we lived.' Streletskaya Bay is a few miles
west of Sevastopol. The Chersonese is the south-westernmost
point of the Crimea. Balaklava and Inkerman ('French bullets'
and 'rusted splinters of heavy shells') are both in this area. Cape
Fiolent lies across the steppe a few miles south-east of the
Chersonese on which stands the ruined Greek city of Korsun
(Old Russian name for the Greek Cherson). Constantine's
battery commanded the entrance to the main harbour of
Sevastopol. The lighthouse referred to was probably Inkerman,
east of the Chersonese. Outside Sevastopol, near Streletskaya
Bay, was the church of St Vladimir. The monastery of St George
was on the cliffs of Cape Fiolent.

Page 72:

Boris Pasternak   In 1928 Boris Pasternak had written a poem
'To Anna Akhmatova'.

'. . . to the cursed, black, Daryal tombstone': the Daryal gorge
pierces the Caucasus and the river Terek flows turbulently at
the bottom of it. It occurs in the poetry of Lermontov, to
whom Pasternak dedicated his collection My Sister Life. In

'About these Verses' from this collection Lermontov's name is linked with Daryal. Also in 'Waves' from the first part of *Second Birth* Pasternak describes it:

> ... he walked with a knapsack along the bottom of the ravine,
> Where the bones of steep slopes and the clouds
> stick out, like the poles of a catafalque,
> and look at the mine-shaft cage.

There is a Georgian legend that queen Darya, who lived in a tower above the gorge, enticed travellers to her by her magical powers, and threw their decapitated bodies into the Terek in the morning.

'He compared smoke with Laocoon': see Pasternak's poem 'Fathers':

> The smoke will be
> like Laocoon
> over the crackling frost,
> stripped off
> like an athlete
> to clasp and throw the cloud.

Index of poems, cycles and first lines

Italic type denotes poem titles
SMALL CAPITALS denote cycle titles

108

III